The Zodiac

Also by JAMES DICKEY

Poetry
The Eye-Beaters, Blood, Victory
    Madness, Buckhead and Mercy
Into the Stone
Drowning
Helmets
Two Poems of the Air
Buckdancer's Choice
Poems 1957–1967

Fiction
Deliverance

Criticism
Sorties
The Suspect in Poetry
Babel to Byzantium

Belles-Lettres
Self-Interviews

JAMES DICKEY

The Zodiac

1976

DOUBLEDAY & COMPANY, INC.

GARDEN CITY, NEW YORK

Dickey, James.
The zodiac.
Based on the poem, The zodiac by H. Marsman.
I. Title.   II. Marsman, Hendrik, 1899–1940.   The zodiac.
PS3554.I32Z35   811'.5'4
ISBN 0-385-02065-1

Library of Congress Catalog Card Number: 76-2767
Printed in the United States of America
First Edition

This poem is based on another of the same title.
It was written by Hendrik Marsman, who was killed
by a torpedo in the North Atlantic in 1940.
It is in no sense a translation, for the liberties
I have taken with Marsman's original poem are such
that the poem I publish here,
with the exception
of a few lines,
is completely my own.

The Zodiac

Its twelve sections are the story of a drunken
and perhaps dying Dutch poet who returns to his
home in Amsterdam after years of travel and
tries desperately to relate himself, by means of stars,
to the universe.

–homage to Hendrik Marsman, lost at sea, 1940–

The man I'm telling you about brought himself back alive
A couple of years ago.   He's here,
  Making no trouble
                    over the broker's peaceful
  Open-bay office at the corner of two canals
      That square off and starfish into four streets
          Stumbling like mine-tunnels all over town.

  To the right, his window leaps and blinds
                              and sees
The bridges shrivel on contact with low cloud
                          leaning to reach out
  Of his rent-range
              and get to feudal doors:
      Big-rich houses whose thick basement-stones
          Turn water into cement inch by inch
          As the tide grovels down.
                    When that tide turns

He turns left   his eyes back-swivel into his head
        In hangover-pain like the flu   the flu
     Dizzy with tree-tops
               all dead, but the eye going
 Barely getting   but getting you're damn right but still
     Getting them.
               Trees, all right.   No leaves.   All right,

Trees, stand
         and deliver.   They stand and deliver
Not much: stand
Wobble-rooted, in the crumbling docks.
               So what?

The town square below, deserted as a Siberian crater, lies in the middle
Of his white-writing darkness   stroboscoped   red-stopped by the stammering mess
  Of the city's unbombed neon, sent through rivers and many cities
        By fourth-class mail from Hell.

All right, since you want to, look:

     Somebody's lugged a priest's failed prison-cell
     Swaybacked up the broker's cut-rate stairs.   He rents it on credit.

No picture
        nothing but a bed and desk
  And empty paper.
             A flower couldn't make it in this place.
  It couldn't live, or couldn't get here at all.
             No flower could get up these steps,
             It'd wither at the hollowness
Of these foot-stomping
              failed creative-man's boards—
           There's nothing to bring love or death

            Or creative boredom through the walls.
                         Walls,

          Ah walls.   They're the whole place.   And any time,
       The easting and westing city in the windows
       Plainly are not true
              without a drink.   But the *walls*—
   Weightless   ridiculous   bare
         Are there just enough to be dreadful
Whether they're spinning or not.   They're there to go round him

    And keep the floor turning with the earth.   11

He moves among stars.
Sure.   We all do, but he is star-*crazed*, mad

With *Einfühling*, with connecting and joining things that lay their meanings

Over billions of light years
eons of time—Ah,

Years of light: billions of them: they are pictures

Of some sort of meaning.   He thinks the secret

Can be read.   But human faces swim through
Cancer   Scorpio   Leo   through all the stupefying design,

And all he can add to it or make of it, living or dead:
An eye lash-flicker, a responsive
light-year light
From the pit of the stomach, and a young face comes on,
Trying for the pit of his poem
strange   remembered
Comes on faintly, like the faint, structural light
Of Alnilam, without which Orion

Would have no center   the Hunter

Could not hunt, in the winter clouds.
                                        The face comes on

Glowing with billions of miles   burning like nebulae,
        Like the horse-head nebula in Andromeda—

              She was always a little horse-faced,
        At least in profile   she is some strange tint
        Of second-order blue: intensity   she is eternal
   As long as *he* lives—the stars and his balls meet
        And she shows herself as any face does
                   That *is* eternal, raying in and out
   Of the body of a man: in profile   sketched-in by stars
               Better than the ones God set turning

        Around us forever.
                           The trees night-pale

   Out.   Vacuum.
                 Absolute living-space-white.   Only one way beyond

The room.
           The Zodiac.
                 He must solve it   must believe it   learn to read it   13

                              No, wallow in it

As poetry.

                    He's drunk.   Other drunks, it's alligators
                    Or rats, their scales and eyes
Turning the cold moon molten on the floor.—   With him, it's his part-time army

                    Of soldier ants; they march over
                    His writing hand, heading for the Amazon Basin.
                    He can take *them* . . .
                                        He bristles   itches like a sawdust-pile

                    But something's more important than flesh-crawling
                    To gain an image
                                        line by line: they give him an idea.   Suppose—

                        Well, let's just suppose I . . .

                    No ants.   No idea.   Maybe they'll come back
                    All wildly drunk, and dance
                    Into the writing.   It's worth a try.

                    Hot damn, here they come!   He knows them, name for name
                    As they surround his fingers, and carry the maze
14   Onto the paper: they're named for generals.

                                                    He thinks
        That way: of history, with his skin
                                        with everything

He has, including delirium tremens
                                staring straight

Into the lamp.   You are a strange creature,

Light,
        he says to light.   Maybe one day I'll get something
Bigger than ants   maybe something from the sea.
        Keep knocking back the *aquavit*. By the way, my man, get that *aqua!*
There's a time acoming when the life of the sea   when

        The stars and their creatures get together.

Light
        is another way. This is when the sun drifts in
        Like it does in any window, but this sun is coming
From the east part of town.   Shit, I don't know where I am
        This desk is rolling like the sea
                                Come home   come to my home—

I'll never make it to land.   I am alone:

                                                                15

I am my brother:

    I look at my own decoration
              Outside of the page:
                              three rods: they're turning modernly—

  A mobile he's got up
Above the bed, from splintered bottle-bits and coat-hangers:

    You know they are, there really *are*
             Small, smashed greens revolving
In a room.
              It all hangs together, and *you* made it:
        Its axis is spinning
Through the Zodiac.
                He flicks it and sets the model
       For a universe of green, see-through stars
Going faster.   The white walls stagger
        With lights:
    He has to hold onto the chair: the room is pitching and rolling—
        He's sick   seasick with his own stars,
              seasick and airsick   sick

        With the Zodiac.

Even drunk
Even in the white, whiskey-struck, splintered star of a bottle-room dancing,
He knows he's not fooling himself   he knows

Not a damn thing of stars   of God   of space

Of time   love night death sex fire numbers signs words,

Not much of poetry.   But by God, we've got a *universe*

Here

Those designs of time are saying *something*
Or maybe something or *other*.

Night—

Night tells us.   It's coming—

Venus shades it and breaks it.   Will the animals come back
Gently, creatively open,

Like they were?

Yes.

The great, burning Beings   melt into place

A few billion-lighted inept beasts

Of God—

      What else is there?   What other signs   what other symbols

   Are *anything* beside these?   If the thing hasn't been said
This way,   then God can't say it.

                      Unknown.   Unknown.
   His mobile made of human shattering-art
  Is idling through space, and also oddly, indifferently,
Supremely, through beauty as well.   Yes,

   Sideways through beauty.   He swirls in his man-made universe,

His room, his liquor, both the new bottle and the old
   Fragmented godlike one.
He never gets tired.   Through his green, moving speckles,

He looks sideways, out and up   and there it is:
   The perpetual Eden of space
                there when you want it.

18   What animal's getting outlined?

All space is being bolted
Together: eternal blackness

                     studded with creatures.

Stars.
          Beasts.   Nothing left but the void
               Deep-hammering its creatures with light-years.
Years made of light.
                 Only light.

                       Yes.

But what about the damned *room*?
God-beast-stars   wine-bottle constellations   jack-off dreams
And silence. That's about it.

                    They're all one-eyed—
The Lion   the Scorpion   the others coming—
      Their one-eyed eyesight billions of years
In the making, making and mixing with his liquor-bottle green
Splintered shadows   *art*-shadows, for God's sake:

     Look, stupid, get your nose out of the sky for once.
There're things that are *close* to you, too. Look at *that!*

Don't cringe: look right out over town.
Real birds. There they are in their curves, moving in their great element
That causes our planet to be blue and causes us all
To breathe.   Ah, long ghostly drift
Of wings.

Well, son of a bitch.

He sits and writes,
And the paper begins to run
with signs.
But he can't get rid of himself enough
To write poetry.   He keeps thinking Goddamn
I've misused myself   I've fucked up   I haven't worked—

I've traveled and screwed too much,
but but by dawn, now   NOW
Something   coming   through-coming   down-coming   up
To me   ME!
His hand reaches, dazzling with drink   half alive,
for the half-dead vision.   That room and its page come in and
out
Of being.   You talk about *looking:*   would you look at *that*
20   Electric page!   What the hell did I say?   Did *I* say that?

You bastard, you. Why didn't you know that before?
Where the hell have you been with your *head*?
You and the paper should have known it, you and the ink: you write

Everybody writes

With blackness. Night. Why has it taken you all this time?
                    All this travel, all those lives
              You've fucked up? All those books read
Not deep enough? It's staring you right in the face.   The
                                                              secret—

    Is whiteness.   You can do *anything* with that.   But no—
        The secret is that on whiteness you can release
        The blackness,
                        The night sky.   Whiteness is death   is dying
    For human words to raise it from purity   from the grave
        Of too much light.   Words must come to it
    Words from *any*where   from   from
Swamps   mountains   mud   shit   hospitals   wars   travels   from

            Stars

From the Zodiac.

You son of a bitch, you! Don't try to get away from yourself!
I won't have it! You know God-damned well I mean you! And you too,
            Pythagoras!   Put down that guitar, lyre, whatever it is!
You've driven me nuts enough with your music of the spheres!
            But I'll bet you know what to know:

Where God once stood in the stadium
Of European history, and battled mankind in the blue air
            Of manmade curses, under the exploding flags
Of dawn,   I'd put something else now:
            I'd put something overhead   something new: a new beast

For the Zodiac.   I'd say to myself like a man

            Bartending for God,
                        What'll it be?
Great! The stars are mine, and so is
                        The imagination to work them—
                                    To create.
            Christ, would you tell me why my head
Keeps thinking up these nit-witted, useless images?

            Whiskey helps.

But it does.   It does.   And now I'm working
        With *constellations!* What'll it *be*, Heaven? What new creature
    Would you *like* up there?   Listen, you universal son-of-a-bitch,
You're talking to a poet now, so don't give me a lot of shit.
        My old man was a God-damned astronomer
Of sorts
        —and didn't he say the whole sky's *invented?*
    Well, I am now in*vent*ing.   You've *got* a Crab:
Especially tonight. I love to eat them: They scare me to death!
        My head is smashed with *aquavit,*
And I've got a damn good Lobster in it   for   for
        The Zodiac.   I'll send it right up.
                                                And   listen now

I want *big* stars: some red   some white   some blue-white dwarves—
    I want *everybody* to see my lobster! This'll be a *healing* lobster:
    Not Cancer.   People will pray to him.   He'll have a good effect
On Time.
            Now what I want to do is stretch him out

    Jesus Christ, I'm drunk
                    I said stretch   stretch
Him out is what I said   stretch him out for millions

23

Of light years.   His eye   his eye

      I'll make blue-white, so that the thing
Will cut and go deep and heal.   God, the *claws* that son-of-a-bitch

      Is going to get from You! The clock-spire is telling me
To lie

      for glory.   This is a poet talking to You
Like you talked to yourself, when you made all this up   while you conceived

      The Zodiac. From every tower in Europe:
From my lifework and stupid travels and loneliness
      And drunkenness, I'm changing the heavens
In my head. Get up there, baby, and dance on your claws:
      On the claws God's going to give you.
              I'm just before throwing up
All over myself.   I've failed again.   My lobster can't make it
      To Heaven.   He's right here in town.   It must be the DT's.

      You know, old lyre-picking buddy,
You in your whirling triangles, your terror of looking into a glass
      Beside a light, your waking from ancient new-math,
To say, "Wretches, leave those beans alone," and "Do not eat the heart,"
      You know   you know you've given me

24

Triangular eyes. You know that from the black death,
                                        the forest of beast-
Symbols, the stars are beaten down by drunks

Into the page.
                    By GOD the poem is *in* there   out there
Somewhere   the lines that will change
Everything, like your squares and square roots
                Creating the heavenly music.
                                        It's somewhere,

Old great crazy thinker
                            ah
                                        farther down

In the abyss.   It takes triangular eyes

                To see Heaven.   I got 'em from you.
                                        All right,

I've got what I want, for now, at least.

                The paper staggers
From black to white to black, then to a kind of throbbing gold
                And blue, like the missal he read as a boy. It's like something
                            He dreamed of finding

In a cave, where the wellspring of creative blood
Bubbles without death.
Where the hell *is* the light
Of the universe?   Gone out and around
The world.   Oh my God

You've got to look up

again: you've *got* to do it   you're committed
To it   look up   UP   you failed son of a bitch up MORE
There it is
Your favorite constellation
the hurdling-deep Hunter

Orion

With dim Alnilam sputtering in the middle.
Well, but   quiet   why?
Why that one?   Why do you even remember
The name?   The star's no good: not pretty,
Not a good navigational aid.
Ah, but secret.

Ah, but central.

Let me explain it to you: that strange, overlooked, barely existing star

Is essential to the belt

Of the great, great Hunter.

Look.

Just look.   The sword hangs down

The dog star travels on   on like European Christian soldiers going on

Before.

The whole thing's hacked out

Like cuneiform.   All right, so Orion's not in

The Zodiac.   We'll *put* him in, along with some other things.

He should never've been blackballed, even by Pythagoras.

All right, friend, my friend myself, feel friendly

Toward yourself.   It's possible, you know.   One more *aquavit*

And you'll be entitled to breathe.

He breathes

Breathes deeply.

You know, like me, he says to the sideways

Of the mobile,

the stars are gasping

For understanding.   They've *had* Ptolemy,

They've *had* Babylon

27

                                        but now they want Hubbell
They want Fred Hoyle and the steady-state.
                                        But what they really want   need
                                        Is a poet   and
I'm going to have to be it.

        And all the time I'm sitting here the astronomers are singing

                Dies Irae, to the Day of Judgment's horn.

                                                WHEN?

                In all this immensity, all this telescope-country,
                Why the microscopic searching
                                        Of the useless human heart?

                        Why not die,

                                        and breathe Heaven,
But not to have to *look* at it, not kill yourself trying to read it?

Except that there's relief   except
                        that there are birds.

There's one, a real *creature*, out there in a human city.
He's never seen a star

In his life, and if he has,

It didn't register.   There's no star-sound   star-silence
Around him.   He's in my main, starved winter tree,
He's the best thing I've got to my west.
                                    When I look west I know
Everything's not over yet. I can always come back to earth.

But I want to come back with the secret
                                    with the poem
That links up my balls and the strange, silent words
          Of God   his scrambled zoo   and my own words
                                                  and includes the earth

          Among the symbols.
                         Listen: you're talking to yourself
          About Time: about clocks   spires   wheels: there are times

                         There is Time
          Which the time-bell can't hold back
                                    but gives
                                        GIVES

Gives like vomit or diarrhea   but when it comes it is

The sound of new metal.

Well, all right.   Slowly the city drags and strays about in
                                        Its wheedling darkness.

                    He looks up
From his paper-scrap   his overworked script   and,

            Work-beast-white, he wanders to the window,
Getting himself brain-ready   ready for the pale-cell-game
            He plays with the outside, when he turns his eyes down
            Into trees, into human life,
                                        into the human-hair gray,
            Man's aging-hair-gray
Impenetrably thin   catching-up-with-and-passing the
                        never-all-there,
            Going-toward-blackness   thornless
            Thicket of twilight.

                    Words.

        How?

A clock smash-bongs.   Stun.   Stun.
A spire's hiding out in the sound   tower-sound and now
          Floating over him and living on the nerve

     Of the instant, vibrating like a hangover:

          Time.

He waits.   God, I'm going to ask you one question:
          What do *wheels* and *machinery* have to do with Time?

With stars?   You know damn well I've never been able to master
          A watch-maker's laugh.
                              Overhead in the midst of Nothing,
Is the very clock for a drunk man.   For the Lord also?
Is it some kind of *compass*?   Is direction involved, maybe,
          Or is it nothing but the valve-grinding
Human noise of duration?   Do the wheels shift gears?
          If they do, then Time shifts gears.

No; no:

Don't use that idea.

It's simple enough, this town clock,
The whole time-thing: after all
There's only this rosette of a great golden stylized asshole:

In human towns   in this one   in all of them—Ha! this is *our* symbol
of eternity?

Well, it's not good enough.

Night.   Walking.   Time.

Nothing.

He goes on without anywhere to go. This is what you call Europe.

Right?   The clock strokes pass
Through him, aching like tooth-nerves, and he thinks

Our lives have been told, as long as we've had them,

that the Father

Must be torn apart in the son.

Why?

He swings up

Through his eyes, and God

Whirls slowly in men's numbers   in the gilded Gothic
Of thorn-spiked Time.   What the hell: Can't eternity *stand* itself?
        Men caught that great wild creature minute
                    By shitty minute and smashed it down
        Into a rickety music box.
                                Stun. Stun. Stun.
        The new hour's here.   He stares, aging, at new Time.

I know God-damned well it's not what they say it is:
        Clock-hands   heart-rhythm   moon-pulses   blood-flow of women—

No.
            Its just an uncreated vertigo
            Busted up by events.   Probably—now get this—
            The thing most like it is Cancer   both in and out

Of the Zodiac: everywhere existing in some form:
            In the stars   in works of art   in your belly,
            In the terrified breast of a woman,
            In your fate, or another's:
                                the thing that eats.

            If Cancer dies overhead,
It dies everywhere.   Now try *that* one out, you and your ideas

For poems.   Every poet wants
To change those stars around.
                                        Look: those right *there:*
Those above the clock.
                                        Religion, Europe, death, and the stars:
I'm holding them all in my balls, right now.
And the old *aquavit* is mixing them up—they're getting to know—
        They're *crazy* about each other!
Where God stood once in the stadium
Of European history, and battled mankind in the blue air
        For domination, under the exploding Olympic-style flags
        Of dawn, I'd put something *else* now:
                                        something overhead.

        God, at your best, you're my old—

You really *are* the water of life!   Look: here's what I'm going to do

        For you. I'm going to swirl the constellation Cancer
Around like rice in a bucket, and out of that'll come a new beast

For the Zodiac!
                I say right now, under the crashing clock, like a man
34 Bartending for God,

What'll it be?
Do you want me to decide?   The stars are mine as well as yours,
              And don't forget it   and Christ
Would you tell me why my head keeps thinking
              Up these half-assed, useless images?
                                        Whiskey helps.

But it does.   It does.   Swirl on, sky! Now, I'm working
With constellations.   What'll it be, Heaven? What new earthly creature

Would you like up there?   Listen, you universal son of a bitch
You're talking to poet now, so don't give me a lot of shit.
              You've got to remember that my old man
Was an astronomer, of sorts, and didn't he say the whole night sky's
              invented?
Well, I am now *inventing*. You've *got* a crab.   Right?

    How about a *Lobster* up there? With a snap of two right fingers
        Cancer will whirl like an anthill   people will rise
Singing from their beds and take their wheaten children in their arms,

              Who thought their parents were departing
For the hammer-clawed stars of death. They'll live

And live.   A *Lobster!* What an idea!   An idea God never had.   Listen, My God,   35

That thing'll be great!   He's coming into my head—
        Is he inside or out?   No, I can *see* him!
The DT's aren't failing me: The light of Time shines on him
        He's huge   he's a religious fanatic
He's gone wild because he can't go to Heaven
        He's waving his feelers   his saw-hands
        He's praying to the town clock   to minutes   millennia
He's praying the dial's stations of the Cross   he sees me
        Imagination and dissipation both fire at me
Point-blank   O God, no   NO   I was playing   I didn't mean it
I'll never write it, I swear   CLAWS   claws   CLAWS

        He's going to kill me.

III   Hallucination fading.   Underseas are tired of crawling
            In a beast   waving claws for a drunk
        Under man's dim, round Time.   Weird ring
            Of city-time.   Well, now:
                                            night hits a long stride.
36   There's the last tower-tone.   You might know it.

Bronze.
       He feels it. The thing hurts. Time hurts. Jesus does it.
                                       Man,
God-damn it,
            you're one *too!* Man MAN listen to me
            Like God listened when he went mad
Over drunk lobsters.   This is Time, and more than that,
Time in Europe.
                Son of a bitch.
          His life is shot   my life is shot.
     It's also shit. He knows it. Where's it all gone off to?
The gods are in pieces
            All over Europe.
                 But, by God, not *God*—

He sees himself standing up—

     Dawn-rights.   How the hell did he ever get home?
       What home?   You call this white sty a *home?*
     Yes, but *look* . . .
            The vision's thorn-blue
                     between a slope
And the hot sky.

                    And now his travels begin to swarm
All over him.   He falls into clichés
Right and left, from his windows! That remembered Greek blue
Is *fantastic!*   That's all: no words
But the ones anybody'd use: the one from humanity's garbage-can
Of language.
                    A poet has got to do better . . . *That* blue
                    Jesus, look at *that* in your memory!
There   *there*   *that* blue   that *blue*
Over some Demetrian island   something that's an island
              More or less, with its present hour smoking

Over it . . .   It's worth it all   worth it and lifted
Into memory
                he's lifted   he rises on the great, historical strength
Of columns.   Look, you son of a bitch, I know what peace is,
He says to his morning drink.   Peace, PEACE, you asshole . . .
Look at me, mirror.   My *eyes* are full of it, of the pale blue fumes
Of Mediterranean distance.   Isn't that *enough?*   The fresh stuff?
The old stuff . . .
              —but, damn it, forgetting keeps moving in   closer.

It's that thing you might call death.

                              The walled, infinite
Peaceful-sea-beast-blue   moves in   in   it has a face

Bewildered, all-competent   everlasting   sure it will lie forever

Lie in the depths in distance-smoke: he's been there
          Among the columns:
                              among Europe. He can't tell Europe
From his own death, from his monstrous, peaceful   fierce
          Timelessness.   It follows like the images
          Of day-sleep.
                    Water-pressure   smoke   crabs
Lobsters.
          All RIGHT, reader, that's enough.   Let him go:

Let him go back to traveling   let him go on   in   onward   backward . . .

Ah, to hell with it: he can't quit.
                    Neither can you, reader.

He travels   he rises up
                    you with him, hovering on his shoulders,
          A gas-fume reader   a gull a sleep and a smoke
     Of distance   a ruined column, riding him,

39

His trapezius muscles in your deadly   your DT lobster's
Your loving claws:
                          god-*damn*   it, he *can't* quit,
But—*listen* to me—how can he *rise*
                          When he's *digging?* Digging through the smoke
Of distance, throwing columns around to find   throwing
To find   throwing distance   swaying   swaying into his head . . .
He's drunk again.   Maybe that's all.   Maybe there's nothing maybe
There's a mystery   mystery nearly got-to
Now   NOW
                          No.
                                    I can't get it.   Ah,
But now he can think about his grave.   It's not so bad;
It will be better than this.   There's something there for him—
At least it'll be in Europe, and he won't be sick
For the impossible: with other-world nostalgia,
With the countries of the earth.   Holland is good enough
To die in.   That's the place to lay down
His screwed-up body-meat.   That's it.
                                    This is it.

40   It's that thing you might call home.

IV

He moves.
          While he's going

He sees the moon white-out. But it maintains itself
    Barely, in   some kind of thing

    Vibrating faintly with existence,   inside a crown
    Of desperate trees.   Image of Spring,

Old Buddy. But where in this neon,
Where in *hell* am I *going?* Well, it looks like I've come to some kind of

      Lit-up ravine—

Well, what on God's earth *is* it?   I can barely make out
    A black church.   Now come on now: are you sure?

I can't cross it.   It moves across me
    Like an all-mighty stone.   But is it *universal?*
    The thing's been lifted from the beginning

Into this night-black—
                              Into the Zodiac.

Without that hugely mortal beast   that multi-animal   animal
        There'd be no present time:
        Without the clock-dome, no city here,
        Without the axis and the poet's image   God's image
No turning stars   no Zodiac   without God's conceiving

        Of Heaven as beast-infested   Of Heaven in terms of beasts
        There'd be no calendar   dates   seasons
        No Babylon   those abstractions that blitzed their numbers
        Into the Colosseum's crazy gates   and down
                                                        down
        Into the woven beads that make the rosary
                Live   sing and swirl like stars

        Of creatures.

                        Well, enough.   He loafs around
        The square.   He might be a cock-sucker
        Looking for trade.   He's got a platform   a springboard
        For himself . . .
                        Nobody sees him;
                                        nobody cares.

He thinks he's sending night-letters
To Mars, and yet he's looking straight
Into the Milky Way   right now he's liking the hang of it—
Now he's with Venus   he's getting a hard-on
                    My God, look at that love-star   hammock-swaying
Moving like an ass   moving the sky along.

                                                            V

          Dark.

Bed-dark.   The night can get at him here   and it comes,
Tide after tide   and his nightmares rise and fall off him
          On the dry waves of the moon.

              Thinking:
          The faster I sleep
          The faster the universe sleeps.
                              And the deeper I breathe

The higher the night can climb
                        and the higher the singing will be.

Bird, maybe?   *Night*ingale?   Ridiculous
                        but over me   43

They're all one-eyed: the animals of light are in profile;
They're flat: God can't draw in depth
        When He uses constellations: the stars are beyond Him,
        Beyond his skill;   He can't handle them right.
            A child could do better.
At the moment I'm passing truly
                        into sleep, a single star goes out
   In each beast.
         Right.
            The eye.
                 The eye, but can it be
That from the creative movement of the first light
On the face of the waters   from Time   from Genesis

The orbiting story   the insane mathematics   the ellipsis
Of history: the whole thing: time art life death stars
Love blood till the last fire explodes into dark
The last image   the candlestick the book and the lamb's fleece
Flame in delight at the longed-for end of it all
      Will flame in one human eye?   Right or left?   Well, old soul,
      What is it?
44   What does it mean, poet?   Is all this nothing but the clock-stunned light

Of my mind, or a kind of river-reflection of my basic sleep
Breaking down   sleeping down into reprisal-fear of God:
      The Zodiac standing over, pouring into
         The dreams that are killing me?

VI

Dreams, crossing the body, in out and around   crossing
         Whatever is left of me. What does that include?   Images:

Monsters.   Nothing else.   Monsters of stars.
The moon dies like a beast.   Not a stone beast or a statue:

A *beast*.   But it can't fall: it's in a gully of clouds,
A shameless place, like the rest of nature is.

At this idea, one part of his brain goes soft
As cloud, so the Lobster can come.

Soft brain, but the spirit turns to fire
Pure cosmic tetanus.   The sponge of his brain drinks it up:
         In the place where the thing is   seethes

The sweat of thought breaks out.

It crowns him like a fungus:
Idea of love.
Love?
Yes, but who'll put a washrag on him?
It wouldn't matter; his whole skull's   broken out with it.
There's no sponge, no rag—

Poet's lockjaw: he can't speak: there's nothing

Nothing for his mouth.

VII   O flesh, that takes on any dirt
At all
I can't get you back in shape—
It'd be better to go on being
What I was   at one time or another: a plant
In the dead-black flaming flowing
Round flume of Time.

Words fade before his eyes
46   Like water-vapor, and the seed he thinks he's got available to give

Some woman, fades back
Deep into his balls, like a solar
Phenomenon, like cloud
Crossing the Goat—

He comes back, and some weird change comes on:
Our man may be getting double-sexed
  Or something worse
      or better—
         but either way
His children are already murdered: they'll never *be* until the Goat
  Shines blindingly, and Time ends. Then, no,
    Either. Nothing will ever be.

He says from his terrible star-sleep,
Don't shack up with the intellect:
Don't put your prick in a cold womb.
Nothing but walking snakes would come of *that*—

But if you conceive with meat

 Alone,
   that child, too, is doomed.

Look.   The moon has whited-out the script
                Your hand drove into the paper.

    This poetry that's draining your bones
                Of marrow has no more life
    Than the gray grass of public parks.

Leave it, and get out.   Go back to the life of a man.
        Leave the stars.   They're not saying what you think.
God is a rotten artist: he can't draw
With stars worth a shit   He can't say what He should
            To men   He can't say   speak   with   with
Stars what you want Him to
                            Ah, but the key *image*
Tonight   *tonight*
                    is the gully   gullies:
Clouds make them, and other Realities
        Are revealed in Heaven, as clouds drift across,
Mysterious   sperm-colored:
                            Yes.

There, the world is original, and the Zodiac shines anew
        After every night-cloud.   New

With a nameless tiredness   a depth
   Of field I can't read   an oblivion with no bottom

       To it, ever, or never.

   Sun.   Hand-steadying brightness   Time
To city-drift leg after leg, looking Peace
   In its empty eyes as things are beginning
        Already to go twelve hours
   Toward the other side of the clock, the old twilight
       When God's crazy beasts will come back.
       Death is twenty-eight years old
Today.   Somewhere in between sunrise
   And dusk he'll be bumming around.
                 Now he walks over water.

    He's on a bridge.   He feels truly rejected
               but as he passes,

    Vacancy puts on his head
The claw-hammer hair of terror.
         He moves along the slain canal

VIII

49

Snoring in its bronze
Between docks.
                    The fish, too,
            Are afraid of the sun
Under the half-stacked greens of the rotten bridge,
And light falls with the ultimate marigold horror:

            Innocence.
                    The fish fin-flutter   able
Unable to hide their secrets any longer: what they know of Heaven
            As stars come down   come effortlessly down   down
Through water.   The trees are motionless, helping their leaves hold back

Breath   life-death-breath—BACK: it's not time—

From the transparent rippling
                    European story they've been told to tell
Themselves when everybody's dead
                                        they glitter the water.

            They shake with dawn-fear.

IX

Again, his stepping stops him.   No reason.   Just does.
He's right here.   Then he's drawn wavering into the fort
                    Where the old house stands
On the vine-stalking hill.   The town moat gets with the dawn,
                    The morning loses time
Under the elm-heavy night, and in lost time   drift the swans
                    On-down, asleep.
            He roams all the way round, one finger tracing
A house-size circle on the wall.   The stone trembles   scrambles—
                    Comes clear: here was his room

                    Here his mother twisted pain to death
                        In her left breast—
                    Above that wrung one window on the battle-tower
His father hauled, each night the Beasts had their one-eyes,
His telescope across the galleried desert-might of Heaven.

Far, far beneath the body
Of his boy   the cellar filled with rats. Their scrambling made his poor, rich youth
Shake all night, every night. His face and neck were like sponges
                  Squeezed, slick with the green slime
                  That gave the book-backs on his shelves
            Leprosy itself, and broke them out like relief-maps.
                  The garden, he thinks, was here,
            Bald   a few sparse elephant-head hairs,

      Where as a kid he'd ambled grumbling like a ghost
                        In tulip shadow,
                  The light humid cool

            Of the family maze.

            The garden where he hid the body—
His own—somewhere under the grape-roof—well,

            Let him cry, and wipe his face on dead leaves
                  Over the little bitch who filled, with *his* hand,
His diary with dreadful verses.

      Why didn't he *do* it? That thing that scared him limp
                  In daylight, that he did all night with himself?

He should have screwed her or killed her
And he did—both—a hundred times. So would you.
      Sure, sure. He always put it off.   Nothing would happen.
Too late anyway.   Too shy.   She'd pass right by him in the street,
      Still, even if she saw him, joking with that asshole
      She married, who'd once been a school-god to him.

      Over.   All that's left of her is the dark of a home

She never visited.   There's no one in it; the man outside—myself—
      Is understanding he's in the business
         Of doublecrossing his dreams.

The grave *of* youth?   HA!   *I told you:*   there's nobody *in* it!

      Why the hell did he come out here?

He lays his forehead on the salt stone-grains of the wall,
Then puts an ivy-leaf between. He turns his cheek.

      Outrage. Bare moon-stone. His ear's there
      And the rock prepares.   It stills   stills
      With his mother's voice. He grinds his hearing   53

Into the masonry   it is   it is   it says
"Never come back here.
                              Don't wander around your own youth.
              Time is too painful here. Nothing stays with you
        But what you remember.   The memory-animal crouched
Head-down   a huge lizard   in these vines, sleeping like winter,
Wrapped in dead leaves, lifts its eyes and pulls its lips back

                    Only at reunion.

        He looks toward the window
        Behind whose frozen glass he'd fucked
        The first body he could get hold of.

        Leaving skin, he tears himself off the wall.

Goodbye?
        You're goddamned right, goodbye: this is *the* goodbye.

        "You must leave here in every way," she'd said.
        "When you feel the past draw you by the small intestine

        You've got to go somewhere else.   Anywhere.
54   Somewhere no footstep has scrambled.   Go for the empty road."

"There's not any road," he says to the ivy
Massing with darkness behind him   that doesn't have tracks,
Most of them men's.   They've always been there."
He sees his mother laid-out in space,
Point to the moon. "That thing," she says,
"Puts man-tracks out like candles."
He gets all the way away

At last winding a little more
Than the garden path can wind.   He struggles in weeds,
Cursing, passing along
The piss-smell standing with the stable,
And reads on the first and last door,
Where his father's live
Starry letters had stood, a new

Designation   of somebody once human and here,
Now also moved away, dead, forgotten around too,

His long name harder than time.

X   Tenderness, ache on me,   and lay your neck
On the slight shoulder-breathing of my arm . . .
There's nobody to be tender with—
This man has given up
On anything stronger than he is.

He's traveled everywhere
But no place has ever done any good.
What does his soul matter, saved like a Caesar-headed goldpiece,
When the world's dying?

He goes to the window,
Hating everything, worn out, looking into the shook heart
Of the city.

Yet the stairwell hammers lightly
Alive: a young step, nimble as foxfire,
And the vital shimmer of a real face
Backs-off the white of the room.

He closes his eyes, for the voice.
"My head is paralyzed with longing—"

He is quiet, but his arm is with her   around
　　Her belly and tailbone.
His heart broods: he knows that nothing,
　　Even love, can kill off his lonesomeness.

　　　Twilight passes, then night.

Their bodies are found by the dawn, their souls
　　Fallen from them, left in the night
Of patterns   the night that's just finished
　　Overwhelming the earth.

　　　Fading   fading   faded . . .

They lie like the expanding universe.

　　　Too much light.   Too much love.

XI

A big room, a high one;
His first time in somebody else's.
Past the window, wind and rain
Paper-chasing each other to death,

And in the half-light one of Kandinsky's paintings
Squeezes art's blood out of the wallpaper.
His friend's voice rolls in his brain,
Rolls over and over
Joyfully, rapid-fire.   The lamp seeps on;
He thaws, forge-red like the stove,
Going blue with room-smoke—
And he shakes free of two years of wandering
Like melting-off European snows.

He tells.

He polar-bears through the room.
When he turns, a great grin breaks out.

The bottle pops its cork, and talk rushes over   rushes into
        Cheese and gin   women   politics—
All changed   all the same . . .
                    Getting darker,
And by God, there's the *fish* market, gleaming its billion scales
        Upward to him through the window.
                            More lights go on.
     Where was he this time last year? He sees it:
Sees himself for a second at the Tetuan Friday Market,
And the *chalif*, through a double shine of trumpets,
       Go into the tiny mosque.   It's all in pictures
In his friend's drunk-book.   He feels his last year, and his back
       To the foreign wall. He turns page after page
         Of the world   the post-cards he's sent,
     Eagerly, desperately, looking for himself,
Tired, yellow with jaundice as an old portrait,
                     and something—

     That's it.   He's just heard an accordion:
      Two squeezed-lung, last-ditch
         First-ditch Dutch chords

     And he's back home.

XII   A day like that.   But afterwards the fire
Comes straight down through the roof, white-lightning nightfall,
A face-up flash. Poetry. Triangular eyesight. It draws his
fingers together at the edge
Around a pencil.   He crouches bestially,
        The darkness stretched out on the waters
    Pulls back, humming Genesis. From wave-stars lifts
            A single island wild with sunlight,
        The white sheet of paper in the room.

He's far out and far in, his hands in a field of snow.
    He's making a black horizon with all the moves
    Of his defeated body. The virgin sheet becomes
More and more his, more and more another mistake,

But now, *now*
            Oh God you rocky landscape   give me,   Give
Me drop by drop
            desert water at least.

I want now to write about deserts

And in the dark the sand begins to cry
For living water that not a sun or star
Can kill, and for the splay camel-prints that bring men,
And the ocean with its enormous crooning, begs

For haunted sailors   for refugees putting back
Flesh on their ever-tumbling bones
To man that fleet,
for in its ships
Only, the sea becomes the sea.

Oh my own soul, put me in a solar boat.
Come into one of these hands
Bringing quietness and the rare belief
That I can steer this strange craft to the morning
Land that sleeps   in the universe on all horizons
And give this home-come man who listens in his room

To the rush and flare of his father
Drawn at the speed of light to Heaven
Through the wrong end of his telescope, expanding the universe,

The instrument   the tuning-fork—
He'll flick it with his bandless wedding-finger—
Which at a touch reveals the form
Of the time-loaded European music
That poetry has never really found,
Undecipherable as God's bad, Heavenly sketches,
Involving fortress and flower, vine and wine and bone,

And shall vibrate through the western world
So long as the hand can hold its island
Of blazing paper, and bleed for its images:
Make what it can of what is:

So long as the spirit hurls on space
The star-beasts of intellect and madness.